I'd Bark but You Never Listen

AN ILLUSTRATED GUIDE TO THE JEWISH DOG

Harold Kimmel

Red Rock Press

I'D BARK BUT YOU NEVER LISTEN
An Illustrated Guide to the Jewish Dog

Copyright © 2008 Harold Kimmel

ISBN: 9781933176-22-2

LCCN: 2007940337

Red Rock Press
New York, New York

www.redrockpress.com

Printed in Singapore

*This book is dedicated to my daughter, Rachel,
who has always allowed me to take the side
of the restaurant booth looking out.*

A dog will fetch your slippers.
A Jewish dog will manufacture your slippers
in China and have them shipped to you.

Jewish border collies have been bred for generations to keep a bakery line moving without incident.

A Jewish dog can best be taught to sit by explaining the alternative is to stand.

You'll never see a Jewish dog wearing booties.
But occasionally, on the upper west side of Manhattan,
you will see one wearing Birkenstocks.

Dogs are afraid they'll be left home alone.
Jewish dogs are afraid they'll be left home alone
with a box of Mallomars.

A Jewish dog will always bury the bone the next day.
The stone goes up within a year.

Lassie Come Home was about a Jewish collie
whose freshman year at Brandeis turned into
one long phone call from his mother.

A Jewish dog loves a fire hydrant because—God forbid—
if there's a fire, that's where you want to be.

Poodles like to go the groomer once a month.
Jewish poodles like to come home from
the groomer once a month.

MAISON D'IRA

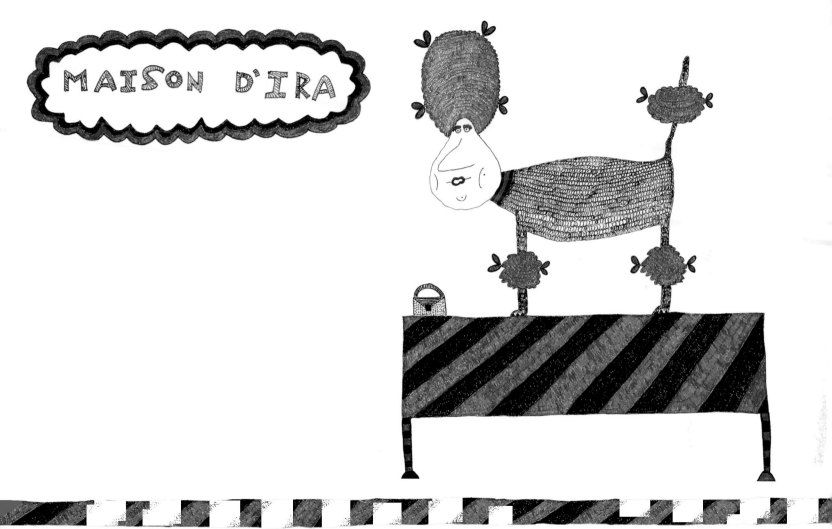

THE
ABE RACKOFF
OVERHEAD SPRINKLERS

OBEDIENCE SCHOOL

THIS SPACE
AVAILABLE.
CONTACT
FRONT DESK.

CAUTION: YETTA BLATT
MEMORIAL DOORS OPEN OUT

PEARL SCHWARTZ
MEMORIAL
DEDICATED BY
MAX AND ROSE WEINERMAN
IN HONOR OF
SYLVIA ZELLNICK
FROM HER CHILDREN
SAM, LEAH, CHARLES, TINA AND GREG

THE
SHLOFMITZ FAMILY
POLLEN-FREE GARDEN
←

A dog goes to obedience school.

A Jewish dog goes to The Milton and Fern Krumholtz
Building at The Norman and Becky Guttstein Campus of
The Lenny and Shirley Zugman Educational Center.
In Loving Memory of Pearl Schwartz.
An Inspiration to us all.

SOL SHENKER
STAIRWELL
→

MORT LEFKO
DRINKING FOUNTAIN
←

THE
ESTHER SLOTWINER
COMMERCIAL GRADE
HARDWOOD FLOOR

Most dogs dislike going to the vet.
The Jewish dog will prescribe
his own MRI.

The ultimate test of your Jewish dog's obedience training is to get her to heel during a half-off sale at the Burlington Coat Factory.

Dogs can be trained to do all kinds of unbelievable tricks. There's a Jewish dog in Roslyn Estates who can cut a bagel so it fits in the toaster.

WELCOME TO **ROSLYN ESTATES**

HOME OF **BARRY**
THE AMAZING BAGEL CUTTING DOG

POPULATION: LOVES TO EAT AT BENIHANA

ELEVATION: NOT TOO HIGH, THANK GOD

REST STOP NEXT EXIT. FEH. TRY TO HOLD IT.

Your Jewish guard dog can be trained to dial 911 if an intruder enters. The dog will then lock himself in a closet and begin deep breathing to prevent panic and the claustrophobia associated with being confined in a small space for an extended period of time.

Jewish foxhounds never find the fox but if it's a mink or vicuna on the run, they'll get it every time.

A water spaniel wears a collar.
A Jewish water spaniel wears a one-piece bathing suit
with a skirt and a built-in brassiere.

If you put a male and female dog together, they will mate.
If you put a Jewish male and female dog together,
they will order in dim sum, discuss politics, decide on
the best public school district, and then mate.

A Jewish dog's favorite trick is to play dead—
just to show you what it will be like for you later.

A Dalmatian is often kept as a firehouse mascot.
A Jewish Dalmatian will ring the bell
but he's certainly not staying.

A Jewish dog won't use a doghouse but if you refer to it as a "cabana" and strategically place some Metamucil and a deck of playing cards inside, it may work out.

The Jewish greyhound is lean and fast—a born athlete. However, nine times out of ten, even after intensive therapy, he will still bet against himself.

Jewish hounds prefer to hunt chickens.
The really good ones just bring back the breast.

A Jewish Chinese Sharpei bakes fortune cookies that say,
"You don't want to know."

A Jewish dog sheds just before she
steps on the bathroom scale.

A Jewish dog is very good with children
but not more than two.

MINDY AND MELODY KUPFERMAN HAVE A WONDERFUL TIME EXPLORING A WILLIAMS SONOMA AND THEN HAVING LOW-FAT YOGURT WITH THEIR WATER SPANIEL, CYNTHIA MINSK.

A Jewish dog craves constant affection.
Sex, on the other hand, always seems better in the abstract.

Jewish dogs are highly trainable.
Barnum and Bailey has a Jewish poodle who can
drive a tiny Porsche Cayenne while putting on makeup,
talking on her cell phone and making travel arrangements
for the Passover in Bonaire Scuba Extravaganza.

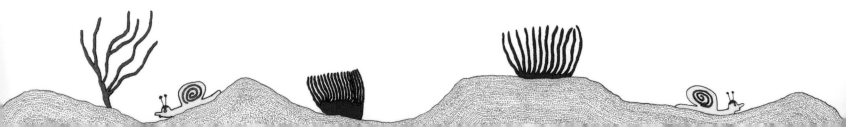

An older dog needs a lot of sleep.

An older Jewish dog needs a hearing aid, orthopedic shoes,

a titanium walker, a licensed companion with a certificate

in cardio-pulmonary resuscitation, a pill-go-round—

the one you get at Walgreens, not the one you get at Rite-Aid,

a home blood-pressure cuff—the one you get at Rite-Aid, not the

one you get at Walgreens, a magnifying glass to read the paper,

a shower cap and a nice fruit bowl.

Call me when you get home.

The rarest of Jewish breeds is the retriever.

It is believed to be extinct.

Jewish Irish wolfhounds feel conflicted around the holidays.

HOLIDAY JOY

THE MINKMANS' FRY LATKES WITH HEART HEALTHY CANOLA OIL ON THE RECOMMENDATION OF THEIR CARDIOLOGIST

RUDOLPH THE RED-NOSED REINDEER DELIVERS GIFTS TO CHILDREN AROUND THE WORLD